WHEN ALL ELSE FAILS,
READ THE DIRECTIONS

Also by Brother Cysa Dime:

How to Offend God and Suffer the Consequences
In Seven Easy Lessons
Or
The Seven Deadly Sins

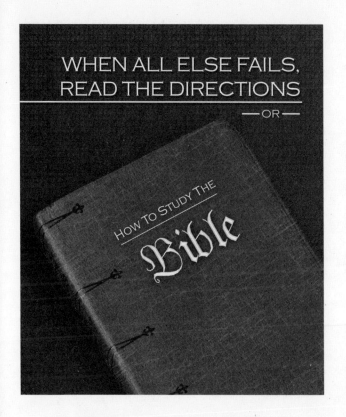

WHEN ALL ELSE FAILS, READ THE DIRECTIONS

— OR —

How To Study The

Bible

BROTHER CYSA DIME

HighWay
A division of Anomalos Publishing House
Crane

HighWay
A division of Anomalos Publishing House, Crane 65633
© 2009 by Brother Cysa Dime
All rights reserved. Published 2009
Printed in the United States of America
09 1
ISBN-10: 0982211902 (cloth)
EAN-13: 9780982211908 (cloth)
A CIP catalog record for this book is available from the
Library of Congress.

Cover illustration and design by Steve Warner

Unless otherwise noted, Scripture taken from the NEW
AMERICAN STANDARD BIBLE®. Copyright © 1960,
1962, 1963, 1968, 1971, 1972, 1973, 1975, 1977, 1995 by The
Lockman Foundation. Used by permission.

The italicized words in Scripture were formatted as such by
the Bible translators to indicate added words that are not in the
original Greek and Hebrew.

CONTENTS

PREFACE

I BELIEVE THAT just about everyone has a piece of the puzzle. If you have spent your entire life in one denomination, especially one local congregation under one pastor, you will find some things in this book that you may have never thought about before. Do not be surprised if you are halted in your tracks here and there.

I have something in common with St. Paul. I come across in writing much more fiercely and authoritatively than I really am in person. Do not get put off by this.

INTRODUCTION

BACKGROUND

OVER THE LAST FIVE DECADES, I have heard and read the most preposterous rot presented by laypeople and theologians, all purporting to get their information from the Bible. I have wondered where all of the Bereans have gone.

> Now these [residents of Berea] were more
> noble-minded than those in Thessalonica,
> for they received the word with great

**eagerness, examining the Scriptures daily to
see whether these things were so.**

ACTS 17:11

In other words, they were praised for not even believing St. Paul without checking the Bible. I was motivated to make use of my spare time to write this book in the hope that a new generation of Bereans will emerge.

This may be one of the few books on the subject of how to study the Bible that is not written by a pastor or theologian. I have spent the last forty years in the engineering field. This has given me experience in observing clues and solving problems. The part of the title about reading the directions is my emphasis that the Bible is a source of information that God wants us to understand, apply to our lives, and incorporate into our belief system. I think of it as the directions for our lives. You cannot pick and choose. If you do you will get poor results. It's not unlike a person reading the directions for a consumer product. When he gets to the section about how to insert the batteries, he decides to save money by not using batteries. He has, in effect, chosen to ignore a crucial part of the directions. No amount of wishful thinking or good intentions will make the consumer product work without batteries. As an old saying goes, "The road to hell is paved with good intentions." It can also be paved with God-words. Likewise, adding steps to the directions will not make it do additional things. Anointing your electric toothbrush with oil will not make it play videos, no matter how good your intentions. God had the Bible written so that we could have a complete source of what God wants us to know. It even warns about accepting additional or conflicting information.

> But even if we, or an angel from heaven, should preach to you a gospel contrary to what we have preached to you, he is to be accursed! As we have said before, so I say again now, if any man is preaching to you a

**gospel contrary to what you received, he is
to be accursed!**

GALATIANS 1 : 8 – 9

And why should we reject such information from
an angel?

**For such men are false apostles, deceitful
workers, disguising themselves as apostles
of Christ. No wonder, for even Satan
disguises himself as an angel of light.**

2 CORINTHIANS 11 : 13 – 14

The above verse warns us that Satan can appear
to be one of God's angels. To help you get the most
out of this book, I have included several examples
and some exercises where you are asked to write
a paragraph and then turn to an appendix for a
discussion.

I have also included illustrations from the lov-
able eccentricities of my colorful relatives and others.
The purpose of these illustrations is not to be disre-

spectful, but to provide easy-to-remember examples that will remind you of the points presented. Also, I use the general term "God" throughout this book for members of the Trinity, individually and in different combinations.

ORGANIZATION OF THE BOOK

CHAPTER 1: Motives for studying the Bible. Several common motives are probably insulting to God since they involve the deadly sin of pride.

CHAPTER 2: Meanings of words and how to find them. This is a larger problem than many people think. It is common to have four-hundred-year-old British words for which a U.S. reader applies a modern U.S., and possibly slang, definition, and derives some totally off-base idea from the sentence.

CHAPTER 3: Tools, both books and software. These are arranged in priority order for people with limited finances or time.

CHAPTER 4: Examples of how to use the tools. There are examples and suggested exercises for you to do.

CHAPTER 5: Analysis methods. The various types of books of the Bible are explained, in addition to ways to evaluate the evidence. Examples are provided.

CHAPTER 6: Common interpretational errors. I have seen all of these over the years. The interpreting errors you are not "guilty" of will probably amuse you. I hope that you seriously think about correcting the ones you make.

CHAPTER 7: Suggested study routine.

CHAPTER 8: Final thoughts. I give words of encouragement to the new believer and old time veterans.

CHAPTER ONE

MOTIVES FOR STUDYING THE BIBLE

THERE ARE MANY MOTIVES for studying the Bible, and some of them are potentially insulting to God. One example is attempting to gain status by being seen to study the Bible or to have a repertoire of handy quotations to impress others. Worse still is taking verses out of context to support your pet ideas. Worst of all is assuming that studying the Bible will obligate God to grant you favors. Some people act as if God were a magic machine: if you adjust the dials properly, a prize pops out. The more precisely you adjust the dials, the more valuable the prize.

The only reason for studying the Bible that God will honor is to find what the Bible says, apply it to your life, and incorporate it into your belief system. You will find in it three classes of information. One is confirmation that some of your beliefs are true. Another is new information. Finally, you will find that some of your ideas and doctrines are mistaken.

It is important to face the cases of possibly mistaken beliefs. Many people cannot admit making a mistake or having a false idea. Yet, refusing to change them is being impolite to God. There are many ways that people avoid admitting a mistake. Some do it automatically. Every new piece of information that does not match their established beliefs is subconsciously ignored and rejected. They can read a Bible passage and "see" what they expect or want to see—not what is there. My late mother was born in San Francisco in 1922 and lived there for fifteen years. The older houses had ceilings that are higher than those built after about 1930. One day my mother remarked that it was always cold in the winter there because of the high ceilings. When I suggested that it was cold in the house from the lack of insulation, she insisted that this could not possibly be the cause—they were cold from the high ceilings!

Others notice a conflict but refuse to admit to themselves or to others that it exists. If this is brought to their attention in public, they may do the strangest things to avoid admission. One humorous hypothetical example is to claim that admitting a mistake is compromise—a compromise that will lead down the slippery slope towards wearing grass skirts while bowing down to stone statues and performing human sacrifices. I have seen less severe examples of this. During the Eisenhower, Kennedy, and Johnson administrations, any official who said that the war in Vietnam could not be won, or was being lost, was demoted or fired. This explains the inflated success rates reported by the military. If they told the truth, they would not be promoted, which would result in their being forced out of the military—many of them without a pension.

LET'S TAKE A TEST

Write a paragraph about the quantity of each animal that went on Noah's Ark and one on the number of wise men that brought gifts to the infant Jesus. Include the source of your beliefs and how sure you are of them. When you are through, turn to appendix 1.

CHAPTER TWO

THE MEANINGS OF WORDS

INTRODUCTION

LET US START with three humorous examples. There is the famous story of the schoolchild that thought the song with the line *gladly, the cross I'd bear* was about *Gladly the Cross-Eyed Bear*. This is an example of mishearing the spoken word. Another famous story is that of the schoolchild thinking that the angel drove Adam and Eve out of the garden in an automobile. This is an example of a word with multiple meanings. When I was a child, I thought that the song with the line *we are weak and He is strong* referred to solution concentrations. I thought of *weak* as a popular powdered soft drink mix that came in small packets. I thought of *strong* as orange juice that made my throat hurt when I swallowed it the wrong way. For years, I wondered why it was so desirable for God to make my throat hurt.

When we come to the Bible, we have problems that are more serious. The original manuscripts were written a few thousand years ago, mostly in Hebrew and Greek. The Bible was first translated into English four to five hundred years ago in England. As is often the case when translating between languages, there are few exact equivalent words in the target language. The forward to the 1611 King James Version stated that over four thousand instances of words, mostly plant and animal names, had unsure English equivalents. So the translators simply made guesses. You may have wondered how Moses found any badgers in the arid wilderness of the exodus to make the outer covering of the tabernacle from their skins.

Exodus 26:14 KJV states: "And thou [Moses] shalt make a covering for the tent [tabernacle] of rams' skins dyed red, and a covering above *of* badgers' skins."

Even modern English translations retain many of the words from hundreds of years ago because these translations would not sell otherwise. People like the old words more than the accurate, modern words. Here we are, hundreds of years later, and some of us are on the other side of the Atlantic where the English language evolved differently than in Britain. You may have heard the saying, "Two peoples separated by a common language." I am reminded of when Nikita Khrushchev told President Kennedy, "We will bury you." The U.S. journalists went ballistic, claiming that this was a veiled threat of war. Nikita spoke British English, and this phrase was commonly used to mean that the speaker would outlive the other person and attend his funeral. Words even have different meanings in different districts within the borders of a single country. Sixty years ago in rural Tennessee the word "carry" was used exclusively to indicate hauling loads in a motor vehicle. It would never be used to describe transporting a suitcase or child with your arms.

Fortunately, these problems are rapidly declining. Archeologists have unearthed thousands of manuscripts that provide information about the meaning of uncertain words. Theologians have critiqued each other's translations so that most modern translations have fewer translational errors. The King James Version went through three or four revisions per century to correct these errors and to update words that changed meaning over the centuries. This caused problems with some splinter groups that got their doctrine from the errors or distorted meaning of words. One such group brought out a version with the errors put back in and claimed that it was done by some anonymous person who was wise and talented beyond the lot of mortals.

We have dictionaries to tell us the meaning of English words. Greek-English and Hebrew-English dictionaries containing only the words used in the Bible are inexpensive enough and plentiful enough that a layperson can afford them. To make them easier to use, over one hundred years ago Rev. Strong put numbers for all of the original language words. You could then get a Bible that superscripts each English word with one of these numbers. The dictionaries have these numbers. We will get more into this in the "Tools" chapter.

SOME THINGS TO KEEP IN MIND

Specific Audience

The writings were for a specific audience at a specific time. The words are to be understood today as that audience would have understood them then. For instance, a farm back then was a family-owned and operated small business. It was not like our modern farming corporations that own hundreds of square miles of land and have employees who drive tractors and harvesters. Another example is: And all the kings of the earth were seeking the presence of Solomon, to hear his wisdom which God had put in his heart. (2 Chronicles 9:23)

This was the known world at that time. The Native Americans of the Western Hemisphere did not send deputations to Solomon. A further example is:

> **He presented another parable to them, saying, "The kingdom of heaven is like a mustard seed, which a man took and sowed in his field; and this is smaller than all other seeds, but when it is full grown, it is larger than the garden plants and becomes a tree, so that THE BIRDS OF THE AIR come and NEST IN ITS BRANCHES."**
>
> MATTHEW 13:31–32

This was the smallest seed known to the farmers in Israel. It does not mean that modern reports of smaller seeds are hoaxes.

Idioms are Different
An idiom is a combination of words that has a different meaning than would be deduced from each word

individually. Do not read the meaning of a modern idiom into a statement made over two thousand years ago in another culture. In Bible times they said, "Verily, verily I say to you" as an emphasis. They did not say, "I tell you this day" as an emphasis.

Mistranslations are Sometimes Venerated

People are comfortable with the KJV and get upset if different words are used, even if the KJV word was a translational error. Exodus chapter 20, verse 13 in the KJV was erroneously translated as forbidding killing when the original Hebrew said murder. It has only been in the twentieth century that many translations have used the word murder.

Matthew chapter 12, verse 40 was originally mistranslated as whale: "For as Jonas was three days and three nights in the whale's belly; so shall the Son of man be three days and three nights in the heart of the earth" (Matthew 12:40 KJV).

Even though the Old Testament of the KJV accurately translated it as a prepared great fish: "Now the LORD had prepared a great fish to swallow up

Jonah. And Jonah was in the belly of the fish three days and three nights" (Jonah 1:17 KJV).

Again, it is only in the twentieth century that many modern translations used great fish. Some people today get upset that this verse is not about a whale.

Joseph's coat described in Genesis chapter 37, verse 3 was a mistranslation based on Martin Luther's German Bible. The coat was very expensive and only affordable by wealthy people. Luther used the multicolor translation because it was the type of coat only wealthy people wore during this period of time in Germany. Some modern translations describe the coat physically as having long sleeves. This means nothing to modern readers who can easily afford long-sleeved clothes.

New Meanings

Words can become encrusted with new meanings as time passes. For example, four hundred years ago, the word "worship" was a secular word that meant that you admired someone for being superior to you in some way. To this day British mayors are addressed as "Your Worship." Since God is superior to you in all ways, your admiring Him is worship. It is an attitude and not a set of ceremonial procedures to go through on Sunday, which the word has come to suggest.

Back then, "meat" was the general term for all food, and "corn" was the general term for all grain. Modern readers will come to false conclusions by interpreting these words with their modern, restrictive meaning.

The full version of the *Oxford English Dictionary* is a good source of ancient definitions.

Foreign Words

The word "angel" is an adaptation of the Latin word for "messenger." Messenger is a job function that both spiritual and human beings can perform. Both spiritual and human beings can be holy. I have seen some offbeat end-times theories that assume that only spiritual beings can be messengers and only humans can be holy. It has only been in recent times that Bible translations have used the word "messenger" in places where it is obviously a human. One clue to which is which, is that spiritual messengers do not receive orders or directions from humans, only from God.

"Church" is a translation of the technical-political word from Greek democracy for a committee that is formed from the general population to discuss a specific issue. This word exactly matches a home Bible study as practiced in early days and today. Sunday school and Baptist Training Union are close. A bureaucratic organization that manages real estate and other investments is not remotely close.

Limited Equivalence Between Languages

Hebrew had a limited vocabulary. There was one word for ancestors and one for descendents. These are translated as "father" and "son" or "begat," even if there were several generations separating the two people. Bishop Ussher, in computing his chronology from Adam and Eve onward about four hundred years ago, used these words as we use them today and so derived what was a minimum possible time span that put Adam and Eve at around six thousand years ago. This caused problems for the early missionaries in China. China was an advanced civilization with a history going back several thousand years further than six thousand years ago. Ussher's chronology was presented by the missionaries as being the gospel truth. This caused many listeners to reject the whole Bible as a false document.

CHAPTER THREE

TOOLS

HERE IS MY LIST of suggested tools for Bible study in order of priority. These are, in my judgment, useful for laypeople. Theologians and pastors will have some of these and other tools.

SOFTWARE VS. PAPER

First, let us examine the differences between paper books and software. Software is lower cost but more fatiguing to read. It also has a tunnel vision effect. You will learn what you want to learn quickly but you will not have the opportunity to be diverted to interesting things on an adjacent page. It may not suggest variations of a word for which you search. If you search for cleanse, it may not suggest cleansed or cleansing.

Books are the opposite. They cost more and produce less reading fatigue. You can save money by buying used books. Bookfinder.com and bibliofind.com are good used book search sites. In selecting books, pay attention to the binding if you have a choice. Older books had very flexible bindings so that when you opened the book the spine formed an inverted "V" with a sharp apex. This allowed the pages to lie totally parallel to the desktop. When you read it, the muscles that focus your eyes do not move much as you read across the page. You will have minimum reading fatigue. Many modern books, in order to have lower sale prices, have lower cost, stiff spines, which cause the page and print to dip into the gully between the left and right page. An old saying goes, "You get what you pay for." Avoid red ink. This is very fatiguing to read, especially for older people and men.

ONE YEAR BIBLE

You need to get the big picture. A *One Year Bible* will guide you through the entire Bible in a year. As you read, have a pencil and tablet handy to write down things you want to investigate in further detail.

I would suggest the New Living Translation for people new to the Bible. It is easy to read, but should not be used to get details of doctrine. Later you can use the New American Standard Bible, if you can find a copy of this out-of-print book, or the New King James Version. I would avoid the New International Version, as it is too smoothly written and will lull you into intellectual sleep while reading lengthy passages. You will see the words without thinking about what they say. This version is great for use with a group that includes children, so it is ideal for Sunday school. I rotate between five different versions every five years.

One of the things you will notice from your reading is that the New Covenant described in the New Testament is a follow-on of the Old Covenant described in the Old Testament. Force yourself to read the tedious passages in the Old Testament. They are there for a purpose. One thing you will learn from them is that when God requires specific ceremonial procedures, garments, furniture, building architecture, and utensils, they are described in painfully tedious detail. Another thing to notice in the Old Testament is that the official clergy sometimes did not do their duty. God had to appoint laypeople to become prophets and warn the people and clergy of their offending God.

SOFTWARE

There are several computer programs that contain the Bible in several translations, dictionaries, commentaries, and other Christian books. These are searchable and are displayed on the computer screen in user selectable formats.

For laypeople starting out, I recommend e-sword available free from e-sword.net. I suggest that you give a donation and get the CD. If you have the space on your hard drive, load all of the files (except for the Bibles in modern languages you do not speak) and download more free material. As time goes on, you can pay for the modules that are not free.

Another recommendation is Online Bible from onlinebible.net. There are some free downloads. To get more of the modules, you will have to buy the DVD for—at the time of this writing—$40. Other Bible programs are slightly better, but cost hundreds of dollars. For now, you have more productive books to buy with this money. One shortcoming of these programs is the search function. It looks for single verses that contain all of the words you specify. More expensive programs will find adjacent verses that together contain the words. Another shortcoming is that many modules, especially the free ones, are drastically abbreviated versions of the original paper books.

PAPER BOOKS

The following books are useful. You will find many of them as free or low-cost modules in the software

Bible programs. Once you try them out in software, you may want to buy a paper version. Some of these may be in your church library or in your pastor's library. You should examine them and get advice from your local Christian bookstore before deciding what to buy.

INTERLINEAR BIBLE WITH STRONG'S NUMBERS

Over a hundred years ago, Rev. Strong developed a number system for the original Hebrew, Greek, and other language words used in the Bible. Now laypeople who did not recognize the unusual alphabets in these languages could benefit from understanding the meanings of the original words underlying the English words in their Bibles. He published Bibles with these numbers superscripted to the English words. He also published a dictionary with the words in numerical order.

There are several offerings of Bibles that also have Strong's numbers in an interlinear fashion. Your local Christian bookstore will show these to you. The one by Paul R. McReynolds for the New Testament is very popular and highly rated. The whole Bible by Jay P. Green is good. I suggest the four-volume edition for convenience. These last two do not have a dictionary. Interlinear Bibles are free modules in most software Bible programs.

DICTIONARIES KEYED TO STRONG'S NUMBERS

There are several offerings of these. Your local Christian bookstore will show these to you. The Word Study Dictionary (Old Testament and New Testament separate volumes) by AMG publishers is popular. Some of these are free or purchased modules in software Bibles. Some of these modules are abbreviated. If you use them frequently, you should get the AMG version either in paper form or as a software module. There are other modern numbering systems, but Strong's is good enough for beginners. There are many low-cost books available that use Strong's numbers. Some of these were written over one hundred years ago and have the problem of containing English words that have changed or added meanings since then.

CONCORDANCE

This contains all of the words used in a translation of the Bible with the passages where they occur. There are versions for most translations. I would suggest a standard type as well as Young's Analytical Concordance. This last one gives more detail by breaking each English word listing into the Greek or Hebrew words that are translated into each English word. This is for the KJV but most of the words are in other translations.

COMMENTARIES

There are two basic types of commentaries. The one by Matthew Henry is by a pastor and describes how a Bible passage applies to your everyday life. Barnes' Notes is the type that discusses the historical background and comments on alternate meanings. Inter-Varsity Press has a two-volume Bible Background Commentary. Some of these are free modules in software Bible programs. I recommend getting all three. You should get your own evaluation of a passage first, and then do a sanity check against what others say.

Commentaries can be used in two ways. One way is to read a Bible passage to get your own opinion and then refer to the commentary for more information.

The other way is to read a commentary through, cover to cover, as part of your quiet time. You should wait until several years of study has firmed up your beliefs before reading pages at a time. Otherwise, they may bias your ideas. Free software modules are frequently heavily abbreviated versions of the paper book.

CROSS-REFERENCES

The Treasury of Scripture Knowledge is a book with thousands of cross-references. This is a free module in many software Bible programs.

HARMONY OF THE GOSPELS

The four gospels present different levels of detail or omit things compared to each other. The harmony has several columns with parallel passages arranged to match each other. This is a free module in many software Bible programs.

SYSTEMATIC THEOLOGIES

These books explain the doctrines of a particular group and justify them with Scripture passages. It's amusing when they describe a doctrine that is unique to them and that is not supported by Scripture; they resort to all forms of contortions and hand-waving without any scriptural references. This effect is easy to spot. Some of the scriptural justifications are not valid, but you should easily spot this after a few years of Bible study experience. It is best to read several books by different groups. One of my favorites is the one by Charles Hodge. He has the defects described above, but I believe 95 percent of what he presents. I suggest using the one volume abridged edition edited by Gross. I also like Calvin's *Institutes of the Christian Religion* with the above 95 percent caveat. A more recent one is by Karl Barth. It is highly rated. It contains eight thousand pages in fourteen volumes and costs about $700 for the whole set. Individual volumes can be purchased separately.

ONE DOCTRINE BOOK

If you want a guided study through doctrines, I suggest *Decide for Yourself: A Theological Workbook*, which is published by InterVarsity Press. This gives the different views of each doctrine and Scripture references for you to do as the title suggests: decide for yourself.

ONE TOPICAL BOOK

About one hundred years ago, Rev. Nave, a U.S. Army chaplain, compiled a list of key words and King James Version Scripture references that were about these words. This was called *Nave's Topical Bible*. More recently, Zondervan publishers has revised this work for the New International Version and printed out many of the Scriptures referenced. This makes it easy to read through without having to go back and forth between this book and the Bible. One drawback is not seeing the surrounding verses, which add more information.

TWO HISTORY BOOKS

The Works of Flavius Josephus gives a history of Israel around the time of Jesus written by an Orthodox Jewish historian. This sheds light on many of the situations reported in the New Testament. One edition is translated by William Whiston, A. M. and published by Baker Book House.

The Works of Philo contains the writings of the first century Hellenistic Jewish philosopher. It also sheds light on many of the situations in the New Testament. The unabridged, updated version is translated by C. D. Yonge and published by Hendrickson Publishers.

CHAPTER FOUR

USING THE TOOLS

HERE ARE SOME EXAMPLES of how to use the tools.

CONCORDANCE EXAMPLE

Some years ago it was proposed that Solomon and the Queen of Sheba decided that the Ark of the Covenant would be safer if it were stored outside of Israel. The ark was taken away by the queen and stored in her country. It was never heard of again.

A concordance can be used to see any passages that refer to the ark after Solomon's reign.

Then Josiah celebrated the Passover to the
LORD in Jerusalem, and they slaughtered
the Passover animals on the fourteenth day
of the first month. He set the priests in
their offices and encouraged them in the
service of the house of the LORD. He also
said to the Levites who taught all Israel and
who were holy to the LORD, "Put the holy
ark in the house which Solomon the son of
David king of Israel built; it will be a burden
on your shoulders no longer. Now serve the
LORD your God and His people Israel."

2 CHRONICLES 35:1–3

Josiah was king about three hundred fifty years
after Solomon. In verse 3, he is directing what is to
be done with the ark.

CONCORDANCE SUGGESTION

Look up the following words: baptize, baptism, sin,
cleanse, blood, washed, and wash. Can you find any

direct statements about what baptism symbolizes and does? Can you find any direct statements about how sins are removed? This is best done with a paper concordance, one that will have variations on the words in adjacent listings.

STRONG'S NUMBERS EXAMPLE

Some people think the following passage means that in heaven we will receive and wear gold crowns just like earthly kings wear: "And when the Chief[750] Shepherd[750] appears[5319], you will receive[2865] the unfading[262] crown[4735] of glory[1391]" (1 Peter 5:4).

When we look up H4735 in *Strong's Hebrew and Greek Dictionary* 1890, we get:

"The wreath or garland that was given as a prize to victors in public games."

When we look up H1391, we get: "The glorious condition of blessedness into which is appointed and promised that true Christians shall enter after their Saviour's return from heaven."

You may have seen statues or drawings of ancient

Greeks wearing a C-shaped wreath of laurel leaves on their head. This is the basis for the saying about "resting on your laurels." In modern language, we will get a blue ribbon.

STRONG'S NUMBERS SUGGESTION

Look up every word in The Lord's Prayer (Matthew chapter 6, verses 9–13).

COMMENTARY EXAMPLE

What does the following passage mean? "Is anyone among you sick? *Then* he must call for the elders of the church and they are to pray over him, anointing him with oil in the name of the Lord" (James 5:14).

Does it mean that we should not seek professional medical help today? Consulting a commentary, we learn that in the first century, oil applications were the state of the art in the practice of medicine. For what it is worth, I take the passage to mean to both pray and seek modern, professional medical treatment. My great aunt took this verse literally. She "improved" the health of her small dog by frequently smearing it with oil. This increased the insulating ability of its fur. Even on cool days, the poor dog would pant its lungs and tongue out.

CHAPTER FIVE

BASICS OF ANALYSIS

BASIC TYPE OF BOOKS IN THE BIBLE

THERE ARE SEVERAL types of books in the Bible. They are grouped by type and are not arranged in strict chronological order. Some of them overlap in time. You cannot automatically apply what you read to yourself.

Direct Communications from God via Humans
The prophets and apostles were inspired by God to write books containing doctrine, direction, and

instruction. You can trust that what they say is true: "All Scripture is inspired by God and profitable for teaching, for reproof, for correction, for training in righteousness" (2 Timothy 3:16).

Narrative History and Biography

There are books of narrative history and biography. These contain some things that you should not believe or apply to your life, such as statements made by Satan or demons. These are easy to spot. What you can learn from them is that Satan believes in the existence of God, but merely believing in the existence of God does not grant him, or us, salvation. A secular example is that having the academic knowledge that smoking cigarettes can give you cancer will not keep you from contracting cancer if you continue to smoke.

They contain examples of wicked behavior that we should not copy, such as King David arranging for Uriah to be killed in battle. These passages are frequently followed by a prophet showing up with condemnation of the behavior. By reading further on you can spot these.

Poetry

There are books of poetry. Be careful about taking flowery statements literally. I do not think that the mountains skipped like rams in a literal sense. Can you imagine the earthquake damage that would result from their literally skipping?

Wisdom Literature

There is wisdom literature of pithy sayings. Some of these seem to conflict if interpreted the wrong way. Modern examples are "look before you leap" and "strike while the iron is hot." However, each one will be helpful if applied at the right time. An example of how these do not conflict is in examining a job offer in the newspaper. You should first inquire into the working conditions before applying for the job. After that, you should not procrastinate in your application because someone else may get the job before you apply.

Who is the Audience for the Passage?

Some passages are for specific individuals. We can still derive basic principles from them, but should not literally follow the directions in the passage. Naaman was directed to dip seven times in the Jordan to cure his leprosy. Anyone else trying this will probably derive no health benefits. With the current state of water pollution, one may contract a disease from the procedure.

Some passages are for specific groups. There was a group of people called Nazarites under the Old Covenant. Samson is one famous example. One of their features was not cutting their hair. Haircuts are allowed for everyone else then and now.

What Time Period is Involved?

Some passages are for a specific time period. The Old Covenant dress code is no longer in force today. One aspect of this code was to wear clothes of fabrics made only from one source, such as just flax or just wool.

METAPHORS

A metaphor conveys information in an easy to remember, compact way. When we are commanded to be like doves, it does not mean that we should lay eggs and sit on statues.

USE YOUR HEAD FOR MORE THAN A HAT RACK

A little bit of logic goes a long way. Read the following passage:

> But when ye shall see the abomination of desolation, spoken of by Daniel the prophet, standing where it ought not, (let him that readeth understand,) then let them that be in Judaea flee to the mountains: And let him

that is on the housetop not go down into
the house, neither enter *therein*, to take any
thing out of his house:

And let him that is in the field not turn
back again for to take up his garment.

MARK 13:14–16 KJV

Some people think that this describes the
Roman siege of Jerusalem in A.D. 70. Let us think
this through. The Roman army surrounds the city
walls and stays there for months. The Roman army
was the most effective fighting force in the world
at that time. For about the previous hundred years,
there had been Israeli guerilla wars against them.
Some of these were successful. If you lived back
then, would you think that this siege portended danger and it was time to escape? Then the city wall is
breached and the Romans kill many people in their
path. If you lived back then, would this cause you
alarm? Then the Romans go to the temple, loot
it, and tear it down. You would be dim, indeed, if
you had to be reminded that Roman soldiers in the

temple meant danger. The warning is given because something will happen that does not look dangerous on the surface. Notice the key phrase "the abomination of desolation." Since Daniel is mentioned, we turn to that book:

And he will make a firm covenant with the many for one week [seven years],
[The Antichrist will bring peace and allow the Orthodox Jews to set up the Old Testament sacrificial system in the temple.]

but in the middle of the week he will put a stop to sacrifice and grain offering;
[After three-and-a-half years, the treaty will be broken.]

and on the wing of abominations will come one who makes desolate,
[The Antichrist will persecute the Jews and Christians.]

even until a complete destruction,
[This will be done thoroughly and with vigor.]

one that is decreed, is poured out on the
one who makes desolate. (Daniel 9:27)
[This will continue as long as God allows it.]

Notice the repetition of the key words *abomination* and *desolation*. This is more reasonable. There is a covenant of peace. People are not expecting danger. Then the daily services in the tabernacle are interfered with. From this point things are going to evolve rapidly. You will need advanced warning to escape the danger. For this prophecy to come true, the temple must exist. The Antichrist will do these horrific things in the future.

LEVELS OF CERTAINTY

Unambiguous Direct, Universal Statements
Some verses are so clear and universal that there is no uncertainty in what they mean and to whom

they apply. Two examples are: 1) "For all have sinned and fall short of the glory of God" (Romans 3:23), and 2) "For God so loved the world, that He gave His only begotten Son, that whoever believes in Him shall not perish, but have eternal life" (John 3:16).

Unambiguous Indirect Statements
Some verses are directed to one individual or group but illustrates a concept that applies to everyone.

> But it greatly displeased Jonah [that
> Nineveh repented] and he became angry.
> He prayed to the LORD and said, "Please
> LORD, was not this what I said while I
> was still in my *own* country? Therefore in
> order to forestall this I fled to Tarshish,
> for I knew that You are a gracious and
> compassionate God, slow to anger and
> abundant in loving kindness, and one who
> relents concerning calamity. Therefore
> now, O LORD, please take my life from me,

for death is better to me than life." The
LORD said, "Do you have good reason to
be angry?"

JONAH 4:1-4

Jonah gets gently rebuked for disapproving of
what God does. We lesser mortals should totally
avoid disapproving of anything that God does. Some
people refuse to consider any scriptural basis for the
doctrine of predestination because they disapprove
of the possibility that God would not predestine
everyone.

Ambiguous or Unclear Statements

There are cases of statements that we cannot understand. I suspect that this is because we mortals do not
have the smarts to understand any additional descrip-
tions. One example is this: "Therefore I say to you,
any sin and blasphemy shall be forgiven people, but
blasphemy against the Spirit shall not be forgiven.
Whoever speaks a word against the Son of Man, it

shall be forgiven him; but whoever speaks against the Holy Spirit, it shall not be forgiven him, either in this age or in the age to come" (Matthew 12:31–2).

We are not told the details of this sin. This has been a matter of speculation for laypeople and theologians for centuries. Another example is: "And then He will send forth the angels, and will gather together His elect from the four winds, from the farthest end of the earth to the farthest end of heaven" (Mark 13:27).

What is the meaning of winds and heaven? Are the souls of people stored in some distant part of the universe? Are other planets inhabited? We do not know and we are not told.

Compare Scripture with Scripture
In all cases, do comparisons with other Scripture to keep from making interpretational errors. For example: "If we confess our sins, He is faithful and righteous to forgive us our sins and to cleanse us from all unrighteousness" (1 John 1:9).

This may lead some to think that they can sin with impunity as long as they ask for forgiveness. The following two verses say otherwise: 1) "May it never be! How shall we who died to sin still live in it?" (Romans 6:2), and 2) "What then? Shall we sin because we are not under law but under grace? May it never be!" (Romans 6:15).

An Old Testament example involving King David is: "Why have you despised the word of the LORD by doing evil in His sight? You have struck down Uriah the Hittite with the sword, have taken his wife to be your wife, and have killed him with the sword of the sons of Ammon. Now therefore, the sword shall never depart from your house, because you have despised Me and have taken the wife of Uriah the Hittite to be your wife" (2 Samuel 12:9–10).

This prophecy was fulfilled even though David asked and received forgiveness for his sin. The rest of David's life was lived in misery. I know of a fellow who planned several weeks in advance to be immoral with a woman and then attend confession.

If he had contracted a sexual disease, he would still have it after confession. Let us hope that he realized the folly of his ways in time and refrained from doing it.

You should always compare Scripture to Scripture to the maximum possible extent before coming to any conclusions. Look for verses that oppose your conclusions. Use a concordance to look for key words and the *Treasury of Scripture Knowledge* to find parallel passages.

UNFULFILLED PROPHECY

There is unfulfilled prophecy. For example: "On that day the LORD made a covenant with Abram, saying, 'To your descendants I have given this land, From the river of Egypt as far as the great river, the river Euphrates'" (Genesis 15:18).

Another example of unfulfilled prophecy: "From the wilderness and this Lebanon, even as far as the great river, the river Euphrates, all the land of the

Hittites, and as far as the Great Sea toward the setting of the sun will be your territory" (Joshua 1:4).

Also consider: "It continued to Azmon and proceeded to the brook [or river] of Egypt, and the border ended at the sea. This shall be your south border" (Joshua 15:4).

Israel has never extended from the Nile to the Euphrates Rivers. In today's political environment, it is unlikely that this will occur in the near future.

In that day there will be a highway from Egypt to Assyria, and the Assyrians will come into Egypt and the Egyptians into Assyria, and the Egyptians will worship with the Assyrians. In that day Israel will be the third *party* with Egypt and Assyria, a blessing in the midst of the earth, whom the LORD of hosts has blessed, saying, "Blessed is Egypt My people, and Assyria the work of My hands, and Israel My inheritance."

ISAIAH 19:23–25

Again, this has never occurred and, in today's political environment, it is unlikely that this will occur at any time soon.

Since prophecy is certain, these conditions must be fulfilled before the end times can start. I suspect that the end times are, at a minimum, a few hundred years away. Over the past thousand years, great social harm has been caused by thinking that the end times will start in the near future. A thousand years ago, they ceased maintaining buildings because the end times that were thought to be a few years away would make this a wasted labor. After a hundred years, they finally realized that the end times were in the future and the next generation was saddled with the cost of one hundred years of deferred maintenance on the buildings. Today many people think that if they believe that the end times are near, it absolves them of their responsibility of being the salt of the earth by voting.

Matthew 5:13 states: "You are the salt of the earth; but if the salt has become tasteless, how can it be made salty *again*? It is no longer good for any-thing, except to be thrown out and trampled under foot by men."

Even if you do not think either candidate is per-fect, you should vote for the one who is the least theologically unrighteous. Too many unrighteous people vote for an unrighteous candidate that will give them the most spoils at the expense of the rest of society. My belief is that at the final judgment for rewards, voting will be one of the criteria for judgment.

FULFILLED PROPHECY

There is fulfilled prophecy: "And I will make you a great nation, And I will bless you, And make your name great; And so you shall be a blessing; And I will bless those who bless you, And the one who curses you I will curse. And in you all the families of the earth will be blessed" (Genesis 12:2–3).

This was told to Abraham when he and his wife were elderly and childless. This prophecy was fulfilled in Old Testament times, and millions of identifiable descendents of his exist today. Nations like Spain that harmed the Jews went from a major world power to an economically depressed country.

LITERAL OR FIGURATIVE?

There are prophecies that may be literal or figurative. We do not know, but our salvation is not dependent on accurately knowing the details of the future.

Revelation 9:16–17 states: "The number of the armies of the horsemen was two hundred million; I heard the number of them. And this is how I saw in the vision the horses and those who sat on them: *the riders* had breastplates *the color* of fire and of hyacinth and of brimstone; and the heads of the horses are like the heads of lions; and out of their mouths proceed fire and smoke and brimstone."

Before the industrial revolution, people thought that the horses were literal or supernatural. In more recent times people thought they were symbolic of military vehicles that shot napalm or artillery rounds.

If this prophecy is fulfilled a few hundred years or more into the future, when the petroleum and coal reserves have been used up, they may be literal or supernatural horses. This would explain the U.S. not being mentioned in prophecies about the last days. You cannot transport enough troops across the Atlantic in sailing ships to be effective against a two-hundred-million-man army.

What Does it Say and Not Say?

When you think about a passage, you should clarify what it means by noticing what it does not say. For instance: "And when He had given thanks, He broke it and said, 'This is My body, which is for you; do this in remembrance of Me.'"

> In the same way *He* took the cup also after supper, saying, "This cup is the new covenant in My blood; do this, as often as you drink *it*, in remembrance of Me."

1 CORINTHIANS 11:24–25

What does it *not* say? Do this to have your sins forgiven. Do this to improve the state of your soul. Do this to increase your rewards in heaven.

From the writings of the early Church fathers, we learn that in the first century, the Lord's Supper was an ordinary potluck dinner. By A.D. 155, it had been abbreviated to bread and wine during regular services of Bible reading and psalm singing. The leftovers were given to the poor.

READ LARGE CHUNKS

Read many verses around the main verse you are studying. Information is presented in a coherent argument or historical description. This will keep you from taking a verse out of context. The chapter and verse numbers are a recent addition to the text. You should not rely on them as indicators of complete thoughts. It is common for a chapter to start in the middle of an argument.

Final Thought

If some doctrine is important, it is blatantly stated several times with variations in wording. If there is just one passage about a topic, and there is controversy about what certain words in the passage really mean, your salvation is not dependent on knowing which meaning is the correct one.

CHAPTER SIX

WHAT TO AVOID

MANY METHODS of interpretation are faulty and produce false beliefs. We will discuss the most common ones.

MYSTICISM

This is where your feelings and intuition are given priority over the Bible. You judge the Bible by the standards of your feelings and not the other way around. In extreme cases, the mystic never reads the Bible. Unfortunately, everyone is afflicted with this spiritual malady to some extent. Keep in mind that malevolent spiritual beings and your fallen human nature can put bad thoughts into your consciousness.

Luke 22:3 states: "And Satan entered into Judas who was called Iscariot, belonging to the number of the twelve."

Another way this manifests itself is during Sunday morning services. The mystic will be more interested in the artistic surroundings than in what is being said and done.

CRYPTOGRAPHY

This is using a simple substitution code known only to the initiated. For instance, when "New Jerusalem" appears in the Bible, it really means Trenton, New Jersey. "Mount Zion" really means Pikes Peak.

NUMEROLOGY

This is a variation of the simple substitution code where the quantity of things has a meaning that can be looked up in a table. What makes this so laughable is that the lookup table has changed over the years. When the New Testament was written, numerologists thought that six was the perfect number because $1+2+3=1\times2\times3$. In the time of Luther, numerologists thought that seven was the number of the Old Covenant and imperfect because it was replaced by the New Covenant.

FORCED ALLEGORIES

This is more of an ad hoc substitution code performed on literal statements of fact. One example is claiming that "oil" means Holy Spirit in some passages and not others. By this method, you can make a passage mean the exact opposite of what it appears to mean. I once heard a literature professor claim that it was impossible for someone to write a statement of fact that another person could not make into an allegory of radically different meaning. There are allegories in the New Testament, but they are plainly labeled as parables. In the Old Testament

they are easy to spot because they use plants and animals to represent people and nations.

TAKING THINGS OUT OF CONTEXT

Information is contained in combinations of sentences. You need all of the sentences to obtain the
information. I am reminded of an old, possibly ficti-
tious, story about a person who used the Bible as an
oracle. He would think of a question with his eyes
shut, open the Bible, and put his finger down. The
first time he got: "...departed, and went and hanged
himself" (Matthew 27:5b KJV).

Not liking this scenario, he tried again and got
"...Go, and do thou likewise" (Luke 10:37b KJV).

Read the following:

**What is *the outcome* then, brethren? When
you assemble, each one has a psalm, has a
teaching, has a revelation, has a tongue, has
an interpretation. Let all things be done for
edification. If anyone speaks in a tongue,**

it should be by two or at the most three, and *each* in turn, and one must interpret; but if there is no interpreter, he must keep silent in the church; and let him speak to himself and to God. Let two or three prophets speak, and let the others pass judgment. But if a revelation is made to another who is seated, the first one must keep silent. For you can all prophesy one by one, so that all may learn and all may be exhorted; and the spirits of prophets are subject to prophets; for God is not *a God* of confusion but of peace, as in all the churches of the saints.

1 CORINTHIANS 14:26–33

Was it from you that the word of God *first* went forth? Or has it come to you only? If anyone thinks he is a prophet or spiritual, let him recognize that the things which I write to you are the Lord's commandment. But if anyone does not recognize *this*, he is not recognized. Therefore, my brethren, desire

earnestly to prophesy, and do not forbid to speak in tongues. But all things must be done properly and in an orderly manner.

1 CORINTHIANS 14:36–40

Does this strike you as directions for how church services should be held? Does the last verse about all things being done properly and in order strike you as a summary of the previous verses? Some years ago this fellow was describing his unique, newly invented, doctrine to me in private. When I showed how different passages in the Bible contradicted his doctrine, he quoted verse 40 and claimed that my finding of errors in his doctrine was causing disorder and that the Bible commanded me to agree with his doctrine.

PICKING AND CHOOSING

You need to gather all information on your question and not exclude the information you do not like. As an example: "For the heavy drinker and the glutton will come to poverty, And drowsiness will clothe *one* with rags" (Proverbs 23:21). Also: "Whose end *is* destruction, whose God *is their* belly, and *whose* glory *is* in their shame, who mind earthly things" (Philippians 3:19 KJV).

After writing a paragraph about these two verses, proceed to appendix 2.

AMATEUR PHILOSOPHY

Everyone is an amateur philosopher to some extent. One defect of this is that people, including theologians, commonly invent an ideal god in their imagination and project it on the God of the Bible. I have seen theologians state that a particular Bible passage must not mean what it seems to say because that would mean that the God of the Bible does not share a particular trait with their invented, ideal god.

AMATEUR ATTORNEY

These people try to weasel out of a Bible command on technical grounds. One example would be: "These are murmurers, complainers, walking after their own lusts; and their mouth speaketh great swelling *words*, having men's persons in admiration because of advantage" (Jude 1:16 KJV).

This describes the actions of certain people disapproved of by God. Notice the "speak swelling words" that today would be called boasting with their mouth. The amateur attorney would claim that boasting in writing or visually with flashy possessions is allowed. I have seen several miserable marriages caused by the woman selecting the most prolific boaster for a husband. After it was too late, she learned that people boast the most about what they are most lacking. The last phrase in the passage forbids flattery or being a toady: "May the LORD cut off all flattering lips, The tongue that speaks great things" (Psalms 12:3).

Some people try to flatter God into owing them favors. Several hundred years ago, this was done by putting fur coats on statues of Mary. One modern example is adding extra titles to the name of each member of the Trinity as if "God" or "Jesus" was not enough of a lofty title by itself. Another common thing today is to curry favor with the second member of the Trinity by having the words of Jesus in red ink. 2 Timothy 3:16 states: "All Scripture is inspired by God and profitable for teaching, for reproof, for correction, for training in righteousness."

All Scripture is equally God's word. Red is also the worst possible color for causing reading fatigue.

ADDING THINGS

One group adds something to a farming parable that a farmer would never do, and then uses the added words as the proof of its unique doctrines. I have a study Bible by a group who annotated one verse about worship by stating that its unique set of ceremonial procedures, garments, and furniture was used even though the verse does not mention them. A variation of this is to do what I call the "just to make sure" effect. This is where a principle or Bible commandment is embellished with additional restrictions and each generation adds further restrictions.

Most everyone would agree that it is undesirable to gamble your wealth away and leave your family destitute. Some groups prohibit playing bridge or watching the Indianapolis 500 auto race on television because those things could lead to being a compulsive gambler.

OPTICAL ILLUSIONS

Your mind sees what it expects. This is how stage magicians fool you. If you are predisposed to certain ideas, you will read a passage that contradicts your views without ever noticing and thinking about it. In other passages you will see what you have been told to see. I was involved in the San Francisco Jesus movement of the early 1970s. Bible studies were attended by the new believers, members of mainline groups, and members of splinter groups. Members of the splinter groups would insist that a verse meant something completely different than what the new believers and mainline members saw in the verse.

PROJECTING YOUR LIMITATIONS
ONTO OTHERS

Here is a story about my late father who was born in 1911 and grew up in the rural Midwest. He finished his education at a high school that did not have a chemistry course. In my early childhood, variable viscosity motor oil was invented and heavily advertised. My father heard such an advertisement on the television and pronounced that since he was unable to design such a product, it did not exist and the advertisements were frauds. This is far too common. People who cannot figure out how God did something described in the Bible think that it did not occur. Many years ago, people could not figure out how God could listen to many prayers simultaneously even though the Lord's Prayer shows that we are to pray to the Father directly. Some of them spammed God by rapid, repetitious prayers in the hope that one would get through. Today we have machines, like the servers on popular Internet sites, which can simultaneously communicate with thousands of people.

Either-Or Logical Fallacy

This occurs when several Bible passages describe two alternatives. These could be easily a "both-and" situation. People form two camps and try to figure out why the passages that the other camp uses must be wrong or misunderstood. Frequently their arguments are from their amateur philosophical ideas about God.

Ad Hominem Logical Fallacy

This is believing in a statement based on whether you like the person who tells it to you and disbelieving it if you do not like the person. I am reminded of the Bible verses: "As these men were going *away*, Jesus began to speak to the crowds about John [the Baptist], 'What did you go out into the wilderness to see? A reed shaken by the wind? But what did you go out to see? A man dressed in soft *clothing*? Those who wear soft *clothing* are in kings' palaces! But what did you go out to see? A prophet? Yes, I tell you, and one who is more than a prophet" (Matthew 11:7–9).

I suspect that many people today would not listen to John because he lived a simple lifestyle and did not have the usual ecclesiastical trappings. A modern example would be automatically thinking that some of the beliefs of people who are different from you are wrong. These differences can be in the areas of education, vocational success, geographic region, and time period. They might even refuse to read a book about Bible study because the author has a mustache.

FORCING THE BIBLE TO MATCH CURRENT EVENTS

This goes back to the first century. One of the most recent was to say that the following passage describes military helicopters:

Then out of the smoke came locusts upon
the earth, and power was given them, as the
scorpions of the earth have power. They
were told not to hurt the grass of the earth,
nor any green thing, nor any tree, but only
the men who do not have the seal of God
on their foreheads. And they were not
permitted to kill anyone, but to torment
for five months; and their torment was like
the torment of a scorpion when it stings a
man. And in those days men will seek death
and will not find it; they will long to die,
and death flees from them. The appearance
of the locusts was like horses prepared for
battle; and on their heads appeared to be
crowns like gold, and their faces were like
the faces of men. They had hair like the
hair of women, and their teeth were like
the teeth of lions. They had breastplates like
breastplates of iron; and the sound of their
wings was like the sound of chariots, of
many horses rushing to battle. They have

> tails like scorpions, and stings; and in their
> tails is their power to hurt men for five
> months.

REVELATION 9:3–10

I served in the U.S. Army in Vietnam. Military helicopters do not have long hair or gold crowns. They carry their munitions at their center of gravity, not at the tail rotor. The munitions cause death. They do not infuse so much life into people that they cannot intentionally kill themselves.

Playing "Spot the Antichrist" has been a popular sport for centuries. For some reason, the candidate is from Europe or the U.S., even though this entity could come from any country in the world. My guess is that the Antichrist will come from the Middle East. My late grandmother told me that during World War I, which was fought mostly in Northern Europe, many people thought it was Armageddon. The Bible describes the latter as occurring in the Middle East after the three-and-a-half years of tribulation in the end times. The reason they did not wonder why they had not yet been raptured is because the pre-tribulation Rapture theory was newly invented and most people believed the long-standing theory that the resurrection would occur at some unknown time during the tribulation that occurred during the last three-and-a-half years of the end times.

ISOLATIONISM

This involves only reading books and commentaries that are recently written, and only by your denomination. A famous British author recommended the reading of old books to avoid "the errors of the age."

Some readers may be surprised to learn that the writings of the early Church fathers show that the early Church practiced baptism by triple immersion. The Orthodox Church continues this practice to the present day. All of the works of the early Church fathers that I have read describe only adults being baptized. Back then, they had a strong sense of sexual propriety. Women were to be baptized by a deaconess. Evidently, they did not think that a pastor or priest had special spiritual powers.

Although I do not hold to all of the Lutheran doctrines, I have benefited greatly from reading about forty books by Martin Luther.

1:1 MAPPING OLD COVENANT TO NEW COVENANT

This is mostly used to justify doctrines that are not clearly stated in the New Testament. Some New Covenant feature is claimed to be the follow-on of an Old Covenant feature. Then the peripherals of the Old Covenant feature are mapped into features of the New Covenant. One example of this is to say that attendance at meetings is mandatory. Another is that tithing a specific amount to a specific organization is mandatory. Infant baptism is another. These may be true doctrines, but a tenuous connection to the Old Covenant is not valid proof.

THE END JUSTIFIES THE MEANS

Some Bible passage is claimed to mean something that it does not say because the new meaning would result in an ideal society. Alternately, a Bible passage is claimed not to mean what it says because amateur attorneys would use it as an excuse to disobey God (in ways that are prohibited by other Bible passages).

SCHOOLMEN

This is the practice in the Middle Ages (brought forward to the present time) of using Aristotle's logic with GIGO (the computer term for garbage in garbage out). This has been used to extrapolate from things stated in the Bible to get more details. You may remember the scene in the Monty Python movie about the Holy Grail where they deduce that if a woman weighs as much as a duck, she is a witch. Two thousand years ago the Jewish theologians did the same thing in deciding what properties the Messiah would have. They expected a military leader superior to King David who would lead them in killing everyone in the surrounding countries. They were wrong and rejected the Messiah when He arrived. Jesus was the Prince of Peace who wanted everyone to get along and not harm others.

There are some things that we cannot understand, but we should say, "I do not know" when we come upon them instead of using this faulty logic to get the answer. One example of an unknown is how Jesus could be both God and human simultaneously. I provide the following analogy to help your visualization. Most people think of spiritual beings and humans as being opposites, like east-west on the equator. You cannot be both east and west at the same time. My view is that the properties of human beings and spiritual beings are different, not opposite. To continue the geographic analogy, humans are east-west on the equator and spiritual beings are north-south on the zero meridian (going through Greenwich England). The spiritual beings can sometimes take on an east-west component. For instance, they can be northeast. In mathematics, this property is called orthogonality.

Keep in mind that God is not obligated to tell us all that is happening or exists. We humans would not have the intelligence to understand it if He did. Paul stated this as: "For we know in part and we prophesy in part; but when the perfect comes, the partial will be done away. When I was a child, I used to speak like a child, think like a child, reason like a child; when I became a man, I did away with childish things. For now we see in a mirror dimly, but then face to face; now I know in part, but then I will know fully just as I also have been fully known" (1 Corinthians 13:9–12).

LET'S TAKE A TEST

Read the following verse and write a paragraph about what happened: "So when it was evening on that day, the first *day* of the week, and when the doors were shut where the disciples were, for fear of the Jews,

Jesus came and stood in their midst and said to them, 'Peace *be* with you'" (John 20:19).

When you are through, turn to appendix 3.

Majoring in Minors

In this, you concentrate on your favorite subject, including practicing it in detail and ignoring all others.

Matthew 23:23–24 states: "Woe to you, scribes and Pharisees, hypocrites! For you tithe mint and dill and cummin, and have neglected the weightier provisions of the law: justice and mercy and faithfulness; but these are the things you should have done without neglecting the others. You blind guides, who strain out a gnat and swallow a camel!"

Jesus has a sense of humor. One of my grandmother's neighbors attend every single meeting her church held even though this resulted in her not having enough time left over to care for her children and family. This is commonly referred to as "being so heavenly minded that they are of no earthly usefulness."

Taking Things Out of Cultural Context

There are many admonitions that apply to the cultural context of the hearers. These cultural things do not occur in modern society. In my youth, the church my family attended claimed that the following verse applied to its female members: "For if a woman is not covered, let her also be shorn: but if it is a shame to a woman to be shorn or shaven, let her be covered" (1 Corinthians 11:6 KJV).

They took covering to be a small hat without a brim. Only women of loose morals appeared in public without a veil two thousand years ago. Today this is not true. A few hundred years ago the only women in Paris who wore boots were women of loose morals.

Confusing Cause and Effect

This is doing the effect and thinking that the cause occurred. This is like noticing that people who are competent and licensed to practice medicine are found walking the corridors of hospitals while wearing white coats. If you go to a medical supply house, buy a white coat, and then wander around a hospital, it will not make you competent to practice medicine. Another example is that believers attend services on Sunday. This does not mean that attending the services will give you salvation. Not even performing miracles leads to salvation.

Matthew 7:22–23 states: "Many will say to Me on that day, 'Lord, Lord, did we not prophesy in Your name, and in Your name cast out demons, and in Your name perform many miracles?' And then I will declare to them, 'I never knew you; DEPART FROM ME, YOU WHO PRACTICE LAWLESSNESS.'"

Salvation is internal to your heart; it does not result from physical things such as ceremonial procedures, consuming bread and wine, or getting wet.

Ephesians 2:8–10 states: "For by grace you have been saved through faith; and that not of yourselves, *it is* the gift of God; not as a result of works, so that no one may boast. For we are His workmanship, created in Christ Jesus for good works, which God prepared beforehand so that we would walk in them."

In other words, good works are a result and not the cause of salvation.

SUPERSTITION

This is where you assign powers to things that do not have these powers. Back in the 1930s, B. F. Skinner started his experiments with pigeons. They were rewarded randomly. The reward made them perform the actions that preceded the reward more frequently. This then caused the reward to occur more frequently after the actions. As applied to humans, this effect frequently occurs when some practice, originally motivated by convenience or economics, has been done for years. People think this is required by God or that it has a special efficacy.

In printing books, to minimize reading fatigue the optimum number of words per line is around ten. With small type, this number will be greatly exceeded on a page. That is why dictionaries, encyclopedias, and some Bibles are printed in multiple columns. I have seen a giant print Bible that still had two columns but only had two-and-a-half words per line. Evidently, there are enough readers who think there is something special about two columns that these books sell.

Several hundred years ago, the officials in the Russian Orthodox Church noticed that the priests were extending different numbers of fingers toward the laypeople when making the sign of the cross. The leaders specified a specific number of fingers. The laypeople in the congregations that had a change went ballistic. God would no longer be beneficial to them because the "wrong" number of fingers were extended.

TAKING THINGS OUT OF TIME SEQUENCE

Read the following sequence of verses:

Jesus came out from the temple and was
going away when His disciples came up to
point out the temple buildings to Him. And
He said to them, "Do you not see all these
things? Truly I say to you, not one stone
here will be left upon another, which will
not be torn down." As He was sitting on the
Mount of Olives, the disciples came to Him
privately, saying, "Tell us, when will these
things happen, and what will *be* the sign of
Your coming, and of the end of the age?"

MATTHEW 24:1–3

The disciples ask two questions. The first referred
to when the temple would be destroyed, and then
about the second coming and resurrection.

For then there will be a great tribulation,
such as has not occurred since the beginning
of the world until now, nor ever will.
Unless those days had been cut short,

no life would have been saved; but for the sake of the elect those days will be cut short.

MATTHEW 24:21—22

But immediately after the tribulation of those days THE SUN WILL BE DARKENED, AND THE MOON WILL NOT GIVE ITS LIGHT, AND THE STARS WILL FALL from the sky, and the powers of the heavens will be shaken. And then the sign of the Son of Man will appear in the sky, and then all the tribes of the earth will mourn, and they will see the SON OF MAN COMING ON THE CLOUDS OF THE SKY with power and great glory. And He will send forth His angels with A GREAT TRUMPET and THEY WILL GATHER TOGETHER His elect from the four winds, from one end of the sky to the other.

MATTHEW 24:29—31

Mark has more information concerning the statement given in Matthew 24:31 above: "And then He will send forth the angels, and will gather together His elect from the four winds, from the farthest end of the earth to the farthest end of heaven" (Mark 13:27).

Verses 31 (and 27 in Mark) look very much like the second coming and resurrection. Examine all of the spectacular activities that occur before it. Some groups put the events described in Matthew verse 31 before verses 2–29 and claim that the second coming and resurrection will occur without warning. You will be walking along without a care in the world and suddenly find yourself in heaven.

FLIGHTS OF FANCY

In this, the sky is the limit and logic does not hold. Several hundred years ago a group deduced, from Noah being with his family in the Ark, that their group is the only true representative of God on earth, and that all Christians should belong to their group and hold their leader in high regard. They also deduced that God required them to kill anyone who disagreed with them.

CHAPTER SEVEN

SUGGESTED STUDY PROGRAM

FIRST FEW YEARS

DO YOUR READING in the *One Year Bible* and take notes of what catches your attention. Look up the meanings of key words using Strong's numbers. Use the *Treasury of Scripture Knowledge* to read related verses. Once you have made up your own mind, write your own description. Writing it will make it clearer in your mind; otherwise, you will have vague, ethereal thoughts floating around in your mind.

STUDY BY BOOKS

In this, you go through an entire book of the Bible. This prevents you from falling into the "picking and choosing" trap. Romans is a concise description of doctrine. Hebrews shows the comparison of the New Covenant and the Old Covenant. Look up the meanings of key words using Strong's numbers. Use the *Treasury of Scripture Knowledge* to read related verses. Once you have made up your own mind, write your own description. Writing it will make it clear in your mind.

STUDY BY DOCTRINE

Use *Decide for Yourself: A Theological Workbook*, which is published by InterVarsity Press, as a guide in going through the doctrines. Look up the meanings of key words using Strong's numbers. Use the *Treasury of Scripture Knowledge* to read related verses.

STUDY BY WORDS

Select a word and use a concordance to find all occurrences in Scripture. Look up the meanings of key words using Strong's numbers. Use the *Treasury of Scripture Knowledge* to read related verses. Use *Nave's Topical Bible* as an additional reference. For doctrine, try words such as "sin" or "salvation." For a panorama of history, try "Ephraim" to see how one of the twelve tribes of Israel started out with good prospects and sunk so low as to reject God. God then rejected them. Fortunately, there is a happy ending to the saga. God will eventually accept them back when they repent.

PHYSICAL ASPECTS OF STUDY

Study should be done when you are in a quiet, relaxed mood. Otherwise, you will rush through it and not think about what you are reading. There should be proper lighting for what you are doing. Paper books require more light than computer screens.

FINAL THOUGHTS

IF YOU HAVE gotten this far, I hope that you have been provoked to think. There is one more item.

FOR NEW BELIEVERS

You are starting on an adventure in a spiritual world that contains dangers. Satan and his assistants will try to stun your spiritual growth by making emotional and medical attacks on you. They will give you excuses to use to postpone Bible study. This is commonly called *spiritual warfare*.

Humans are no match for demons. When this occurs, do not try to interact with the demon in any way. Do not even think about the demon. Instead, pray to God for a fire mission. For those of you who are not veterans, artillery is frequently not in visual contact with what they are shooting at. There is a human, called a forward observer, who is. This forward observer radios back information on where to aim the artillery (fire direction center). After the call signs, the next phrase in the radio transmission is *FIRE MISSION*, followed by the proword *OVER*. The fire direction center calls back to indicate that they are listening. Then the foreword observer gives the details followed by *will adjust* to indicate that corrections will be radioed back when the round lands in the wrong place.

God is always listening, so you can give all information in one transmission. God gets 100 percent first round hits, so including *will adjust* is not necessary. God's call sign is *White Robe Six*. Veterans will appreciate this more than others will.

I am a cheerful sort of person with good health. While writing this book I experienced intense levels of spiritual warfare—both emotional and medical. The worst case was waking up the morning after mailing the signed contract to the publisher with a five-inch by eight-inch painful wound in my side that took months to heal completely. The wound had a combination of geometric patterns that did not match any object in the room.

Always keep the following verse in your thoughts: "Samuel said, 'Has the LORD as much delight in burnt offerings and sacrifices As in obeying the voice of the LORD? Behold, to obey is better than sacrifice, *And* to heed than the fat of rams'" (1 Samuel 15:22).

This involves the Old Covenant procedures of animal sacrifices. Translated into New Covenant language, it means that God is more pleased with your following His directions than he is with your going through ceremonial procedures, no matter how frequently or how elaborately done. The New Testament version is: "He who has My commandments and keeps them is the one who loves Me; and he who loves Me will be loved by My Father, and I will love him and will disclose Myself to him" (John 14:21).

You should read *The Pilgrim's Progress* by John Bunyan to get a preview of what you are going to experience.

For Everyone

Your life will experience trials and tribulations: spiritual, health, and economic. The Bible has comfort for that:

> **These things I have spoken to you, so that in Me you may have peace. In the world you have tribulation, but take courage; I have overcome the world.**
>
> JOHN 16:33

> **strengthening the souls of the disciples, encouraging them to continue in the faith,**

and *saying*, "Through many tribulations we must enter the kingdom of God."

ACTS 14:22

Who will separate us from the love of Christ? Will tribulation, or distress, or persecution, or famine, or nakedness, or peril, or sword?

ROMANS 8:35

Then one of the elders answered, saying to me [John in heaven], "These who are clothed in the white robes, who are they, and where have they come from?" I said to him, "My lord, you know." And he said to me, "These are the ones who come out of the great tribulation, and they have washed their robes and made them white in the blood of the Lamb. For this reason, they are before the throne of God; and they serve Him day and night in His temple; and

He who sits on the throne will spread His tabernacle over them."

REVELATION 7:13–15

I expect that in my lifetime there will be a drastic reduction in the standard of living caused by the rising cost of energy and food and from shortages of pure water. I also expect to see outright religious persecutions. To be forewarned is to be forearmed. If you prepare yourself emotionally for this, it will not be as devastating for you.

My final thought for you is: "Therefore I make known to you that no one speaking by the Spirit of God says, 'Jesus is accursed'; and no one can say, 'Jesus is Lord,' except by the Holy Spirit" (1 Corinthians 12:3).

I pray that you can honestly say with me:

JESUS IS LORD

Appendix 1

READ THE FOLLOWING Bible passage:

> You [Noah] shall take with you of every
> clean animal by sevens, a male and his
> female; and of the animals that are not
> clean two, a male and his female; also of the
> birds of the sky, by sevens, male and female,
> to keep offspring alive on the face of all the
> earth.
>
> Genesis 7:2–3

Did you notice that some animals were in quantities of fourteen (seven pairs)?

Many people's ideas are from children's stories that are simplified. Read the following Bible passage:

Now when Jesus was born in Bethlehem of Judea in the days of Herod the king, behold, wise men from the East came to Jerusalem, saying, "Where is he who has been born king of the Jews? For we have seen his star in the East, and have come to worship him."

Then Herod summoned the wise men secretly and ascertained from them what time the star appeared;

When they had heard the king they went their way; and lo, the star which they had seen in the East went before them, till it came to rest over the place where the child was. When they saw the star, they rejoiced exceedingly with great joy;

and going into the house they saw the

child with Mary his mother, and they fell
down and worshiped him. Then, opening
their treasures, they offered him gifts, gold
and frankincense and myrrh. And being
warned in a dream not to return to Herod,
they departed to their own country by
another way.

Now when they had departed, behold,
an angel of the Lord appeared to Joseph in a
dream and said, "Rise, take the child and his
mother, and flee to Egypt, and remain there
till I tell you; for Herod is about to search
for the child, to destroy him."

MATTHEW 2:1–2, 7, 9–13 KJV

Luke chapter 2 is the only other passage about
the manger, and it does not mention any wise men.

Did you notice the total lack of description of
the quantity of wise *men* other than the plural men?
Many people's ideas are from children's stories that
are embellished. Did you notice in verse 11 that it
was a house and not a barn, stable, or manger that

the wise men visited? Evidently, in the time it took the wise men to travel, Joseph was able to find better accommodations.

How you react to finding these simple errors of belief will predict if you will benefit from Bible study. If you give excuses for why there was only one pair of each type of animal and three wise men, you will not receive very many benefits from studying the Bible.

Another source of false doctrine is from "folk theology." These are beliefs that laypeople devise out of their imaginations. These are repeated so frequently that they are taken as true. One simple example is the belief that lions and lambs will be compatible in the millennium. This comes from misquoting the following passage:

> **And the wolf will dwell with the lamb, And the leopard will lie down with the young goat, And the calf and the young lion and the fatling together; And a little boy will**

lead them. Also the cow and the bear will
graze, Their young will lie down together,
And the lion will eat straw like the ox.

ISAIAH 11:6−7

I know of people who rejected what they thought
was the Gospel because of some person representing
folk theology as the Gospel. These rejecters were, as
the British say, too clever by half. They threw out the
infant with the bath water. One common example of
this comes from the folklore description of the devil
being a cross between a human and a goat with red
color, a tail, and a pitchfork. Since this is obviously
false, some people conclude that the description of a
spiritual being is also false.

A further source is from parents with good
intentions. They knowingly tell their children false
things to control their behavior. As a child I was told
that wasting food was a sin. Sometimes these efforts
backfire. I got to know a certain woman back in my
twenties. I suggested that we should embrace and

kiss. She said that her parents told her that all forms of affection were as equally sinful as "going all the way." From this she concluded that we should "go all the way." I suspect that her parents had a different outcome in mind. I declined the offer.

APPENDIX 2

HOW DID YOU REACT to the verses? If you were caused to think about your possibly violating them, you will benefit greatly from Bible study. If you came up with excuses of why they do not apply to you, at least you have good reading comprehension. Unfortunately, you probably will not benefit much from Bible study. If you breezed through them without any reaction, you either need to brush up your reading comprehension skills, or you are affected by what is described in the optical illusion paragraph found on page 72.

These are part of the verses that are the basis for gluttony being classified as one of the Seven Deadly Sins. Most groups avoid references to gluttony in these two and other verses or suppress them altogether. For more information on this and other things to avoid, read *The Screwtape Letters* by C. S. Lewis.

APPENDIX 3

MOST PEOPLE CLAIM some theory about walking through walls. Notice that the verse says nothing about the physical mechanism that occurred. We need to be content with saying, "I do not know" in these situations. I have heard an eminent astronomer say that general relativity shows that there are several extra space dimensions and one bidirectional time dimension, but the world humans see and live in does not use them. Jesus' resurrected body may have existed in all of these dimensions.

You can visualize this by first thinking of yourself standing on the sand at the beach. There is a circle drawn in the sand. Your body is in three space dimensions. The circle is in two space dimensions. You can go inside the circle without walking through it by stepping over the circle in the third space dimension (vertical) and into the interior. People in "Flatland" will see the soles of your feet suddenly appear in the interior of the circle. In the same way, Jesus could have used a fourth space dimension to "step over" the wall of the building and end up in the interior. If you are interested in learning more about Flatland, you can read the book of the same title by Edwin A. Abbott.

An additional example of a Bible passage that was hard to believe until recently is: "But the day of the Lord will come like a thief, in which the heavens will pass away with a roar and the elements will be destroyed with intense heat, and the earth and its works will be burned up" (2 Peter 3:10). Now science knows that the sun, like all stars, at the end of its life will expand in size so much that the earth will be in the interior of the sun before it becomes cold.